I AM

WHO?

AMARNATH AKKI

This book is dedicated to all my well - wishers from whom I am growing everyday in my life , as well as glowing eternally.

To my lovely & loving parents, family.

This credit goes to the upmost person who changed all my perspective , mindset so I can implement in my life.

To my brothers , sisters for encouraging me to do best in delivering a masterpiece.

To my extended family , friends.

Contents

Contents

Preface

Well I in this existence never been able to establish myself for the most upcoming, upbringing movements which i felt really missed out from being very narrow-minded throughout.

Until I found out one day that requirements for anything mandatory things/ goals in our lives will never be just simple , perhaps than enacting to act nothing has happened at all than being plain.!

So under this book I have found all the answers to you , when & where to actually apply solutions from your different types of perceptions / perservance from time being to lifetime.

Acknowledgements

I would like to thank Notionpress.com for publishing my
5th book , previous 4 books have also been very helpful
for those who have gone through it.
To you who is reading , I thank you wholeheartedly
for actually helping me in many ways & also to develop
new mindset for throughout my lifetime.

Prologue

Why wouldn't we always want a happy ending in our lives , than actually expecting that miracles happen in seconds, all the time when we are going through some or other life goal.
To our surprise , the more we intend to tap all the luck, motivation, min, concentration in following the dreams which we are actually craving for but how come we shall give inputs for anyone who is facing the outcome without any intention going wrong at all!
I shall give my word that if you go through this book throughouly , you will find whatever answer looking for...!

CHAPTER ONE

I AM

- - Amarnath Akki

CHAPTER TWO

I AM

I am a Human being too with all the body parts, brain, mind to think, heart to love, Sub – conscious mind to take action without my permission.

At sometimes this bloody conscious mind which has the behaviour of the monkey to act simultaneously without any precise behaviour with fickle mind, at last it gives you the regret feel so much that you wouldn't want to go this grievance once again through the same situation , experience it.

It feels a lifetime for us to realize , get back to reality of stimulating pressure by our wrong doings / choices.

It isn't to break our own barriers of lost hope, faith which also gives us that remembrance by activating a memory which keeps rotating / flashing like a notification inside our brain just to embark, enhance that to come out of enchantment.

What is it in our lives makes us the happiest, whilst only making the appropriate decisions accordingly, but are there any teachers in life that tell us which decision is right nor wrong?

It only depends on which type of perception, perspective of person individually you actually ask them in that whole situation, but really after some time goes by passing, the same person would be having a different answer to you of the cause which you had taken for the effect which took place.

I would inherit that , we all are different from each other it's not that we belong to one family, it's from different background, experiences , culture , behaviour .

Definitely there would be different options of expertise sitting for the life deciding, calculating the terms of life which even they have not gone through , believe me that's a tragedy of events.

It's not said, to be experienced at every given situation to you, always there will be a new person whom will be guiding you through that certain period of time.

Our most loved , desired , fantasised person would always go out of proportion whenever we are stuck in a outrageous difficulty!.

It teaches us to be , oh my dear friend detachment is the best to come out of a thinking where you would be still thinking of them perhaps than the solution to the problem.

Remember it's always good to have an option to back your problem , the solution . There seems to say a go about our lives not yet recite on the one single perspective, perception, nor a single person can solve all the problems in our lives.

It's about like having a better outlook of a better positive thinker, the person who actually gives you the right feel for a enormous outlook for a being which provides a satisfaction, relaxes human tension.

Why can't we have a different approach whenever we are facing an altogether confusing outreach which is actually making us thinking with whatever the options left in our box, which makes you and me to realize that having minimum thinking level of capability for everyone in common.

That is what makes us to think from out of the box rather than to think from the cage which we have only put upon us ever time, we don't react, respond with rage , but with care...!

It's not just that it comes with experience nor naturally , it has actually need to be told, found in our membrane otherwise we will never able to survive in this material world at all.

CHAPTER THREE

WHO IS AN I?

I who actually thinks in everyone's mind, that they need to be successful , powerful, rich, to be loved, make good friends, have to be able travel around the world, I am selfish , possessive, scared to let go anyone who comes in my life.

Perhaps more serious in life than anyone , to be understandable , caring for anyone who cares , hates for no one, still have that soft corner for the persons whom they have in their life.

I who is actually mere efficient for themselves but still requires some being who actually listens to them, nor get to be heard , every time either they cannot be robots just to feed the data , act accordingly.

Well seriously it is periodically impractical impossible for an individual to go through all the emotions , feelings , heartbreak which a being goes through for all their life through this small time period of joy called expectations.

You actually demand the situation , nor the time that it should actually act according to our life goal , perhaps it's for our own well being that this so called "Life " teaches us everything in between a solace.

But it does matter at last for each one of us to be strong in our decision for what we take, sticking on it gives us more confidence, winning probability for to achieve the outcome of what we have actually dreamt of having in our bag for until now , otherwise it wouldn't be waste of time, energy put into it.

For us being so loyal to a specific outreach/goal should have a proper approach , otherwise it just be a other normal failure in time being.

I is being actually looking at all the options , telling myself that it isn't okay to hang in around for long to a specific, appropriate target, person because it actually makes us think only from a small perspective , or a smaller circle.

Only if we come out of that circle we see how big this universe is, see many possibilities individual lives accordingly.

CHAPTER FOUR

WHAT USUALLY I DO?

I look into more often the point of view from their perception , rather than seeing my only beneficial for my optional help nor for my own self help which is actually from other side as well , even though their feeling will be as if they are on winning side , but alas only you know that you are winning rather than them whom have pity on you.

This is how "I" win a challenging situation in my life , it isn't that simple for me to actually make them believe whether or not who is actually on the verge of producing an indefinite down slide of victory.

I engage in lot of silent conversations of whom they narrate their stories to me , rather than me telling mine of my own which becomes your weakness to them.

I more consume perhaps than feed people with my secrets which are filled in my veins strongly as bones including my blood filled with rage , burning inside but I reflect as chilled an Ice.

I failed , yes many times more than you can think from anyone's life which actually makes me feel that why I am the only person in this world who has faced so many failures , still failing which actually equals to learning and making me more strong , stronger each time I fail , perhaps I am not surrendering to myself and letting myself to loose in any situation right!

I am not yet giving up my life right, nor on my dreams, goals. So why should I even worry about losing until and unless I stop trying, even if I see that there is no way to achieve of whatever that I would want in my life.

I will create a new approach out of which , I can make sure that I reach somewhere which actually takes me at least close to my reach , it's like I keep on trying until I win , nor ending up losing.\

I at least try on which , I give my all in which actually gives me so much of confidence, satisfaction to my sub conscious mind , otherwise I would be so regretful that I have not even experienced that part of my life.

I don't even see the result of which it comes either from praying to god, it's like not everything has own it's advantages , disadvantages prior for whatever we actually think of keep expecting , then be so unaware of the situation.

It's simple there is so much competition in this whole world for competing over each other.

I am not at all ethical , to be whomsoever it might be in my way. I don't mind until "I" win , satisfy myself that victory , even make my mind cool that I at least tried to break even all the mood swings, laziness.

Otherwise I would have stayed between these four walls perhaps at last blamed , regretted over my decisions which "I" don't get to revisit to that position, situation.

I would be more disappointed if "I" pushing myself back for getting scared of the end result, or the opponent.

In the conclusion I will be like to myself 'Oh, crap!! Even these are human beings not some extra ordinary species that have some extra special powers given by god to them.

I become very much disappointed some times thinking why did "I" actually grow up in a society where it feels that every time that you have to be accountable to each ,

everyone who passes through your path, nor be so authentically exposed to them that you are actually living for them rather than for yourself by suffocating inner self, in a dissatisfactory situation.

Everyone wants that instant result/outcome which actually makes them so important only in their particular way of thinking even in smallest of movements.

Perhaps even I wouldn't want to get adjusted to any particular second . It actually makes me think that ....

I am getting to their level which I don't want at all, but somewhere on my mind "I" tell myself no it's not right to tell yourself like that.

Because dude you are lucky that this particular situation is teaching you some good lesson out of it so better learn it now to get the better of it in the upcoming situation , you will face it with experience and with confident.

I am literally nothing , just a small dot of being existing in between this whole universe. Our problems are so small , compared to those who have the biggest of them doesn't get so complicated their suffocated mind like us.

Our inheritance is so acoustic that every time our minds are so ready to pre judge everything to the negative part of it's mindset rather than positive mindset which literally gives us feels.

There is room for me to improve , nor to have some co – operation from myself for actually performing well next time in whatever I try out thing in my life related to my cycle of mind.

I want to clear few things here , not everyone here actually be a winner on his own, nor they are winners all the time , nor winning all the time.

It's like the more you win , more pressure keeps adding on to you until it makes you so hyper tensed , keeps your expectations , frustrated that freaking you have to win.

It only makes your mind so childish , you actually forget what you have to do for keeping your tone highly active by day to day activity.

But,

If I keep on winning few times , losing many times it adds more calmness on me that losing is part, parcel of life.

So I actually concentrate on experiencing, embracing, embarking the journey than making some hasty decisions, awful thoughts about my life by not controlling my thoughts over someone's success story.

I may not be a life coach, mind reader for everyone who can actually tell you what you are thinking but "I" may be a good experienced life hacker for myself , many for myself which actually helped me accomplish some milestones with the same mindset.

So I feel that at least by applying some of these small real life examples you can actually achieve of whatever you are thinking that of dreaming it.

I believe strongly in the law of attraction which actually affirm your daily morning with it, you shall be granted by it only if you work toward it efficiently, loyally, with purest of heart only.

The amount of thoughts "I" have harvested till now has actually come into plantation process where all the efforts I have put on it has actually worked accordingly.

I am working so consistently on it that I am not worried at all how will it grow, does it give fruit properly, to be frank I am not all thinking of the result "I" am only taking care of it without my self esteem , without expecting anything from it in return.

That's how I deal through whenever I see some problem arising to me , nor facing .

I just think of the process by nature for how it behaves accordingly to my behaviour so I can take rightful action in my life with rightful example so I won't be annoying myself or anyone in the progress of my life.

Trust me this second is very precious , every second the karma keeps hitting you back with the same behaviour of your very own applicability.

If someone is willing to listen to you completely by trusting in your life ideas , it gives them strong motto to build good bond, feelings, emotions with you.

Otherwise you will be just another person in their life rather than an 'Important person".

Think which option you would want to choose in those two, choice is yours, so does the outcome also hits you so badly.

Choose wisely.

Experience widely..!
I look into more often the point of view from their perception , rather than seeing my only beneficial for my optional help nor for my own self help which is actually from other side as well , even though their feeling will be as if they are on winning side , but alas only you know that you are winning rather than them whom have pity on you.
This is how "I" win a challenging situation in my life , it isn't that simple for me to actually make them believe whether or not who is actually on the verge of producing an indefinite down slide of victory.
I engage in lot of silent conversations of whom they narrate their stories to me , rather than me telling mine of my own which becomes your weakness to them.
I more consume perhaps than feed people with my secrets which are filled in my veins strongly as bones including my blood filled with rage , burning inside but I reflect as chilled an Ice.
I failed , yes many times more than you can think from anyone's life which actually makes me feel that why I am the only person in this world who has faced so many failures , still failing which actually equals to learning and making me more strong , stronger each time I fail , perhaps I am not surrendering to myself and letting myself to loose in any situation right!
I am not yet giving up my life right, nor on my dreams, goals. So why should I even worry about losing until and unless I stop trying, even if I see that there is no way to achieve of whatever that I would want in my life.
I will create a new approach out of which , I can make sure that I reach somewhere which actually takes me at

least close to my reach , it's like I keep on trying until I win , nor ending up losing.\

I at least try on which , I give my all in which actually gives me so much of confidence, satisfaction to my sub conscious mind , otherwise I would be so regretful that I have not even experienced that part of my life.

I don't even see the result of which it comes either from praying to god, it's like not everything has own it's advantages , disadvantages prior for whatever we actually think of keep expecting , then be so unaware of the situation.

It's simple there is so much competition in this whole world for competing over each other.

I am not at all ethical , to be whomsoever it might be in my way. I don't mind until "I" win , satisfy myself that victory , even make my mind cool that I at least tried to break even all the mood swings, laziness.

Otherwise I would have stayed between these four walls perhaps at last blamed , regretted over my decisions which "I" don't get to revisit to that position, situation.

I would be more disappointed if "I" pushing myself back for getting scared of the end result, or the opponent.

In the conclusion I will be like to myself 'Oh, crap!! Even these are human beings not some extra ordinary species that have some extra special powers given by god to them.

I become very much disappointed some times thinking why did "I" actually grow up in a society where it feels that every time that you have to be accountable to each , everyone who passes through your path, nor be so authentically exposed to them that you are actually living for them rather than for yourself by suffocating inner self, in a dissatisfactory situation.

Everyone wants that instant result/outcome which actually makes them so important only in their particular way of thinking even in smallest of movements.

Perhaps even I wouldn't want to get adjusted to any particular second . It actually makes me think that ....

I am getting to their level which I don't want at all, but somewhere on my mind "I" tell myself no it's not right to tell yourself like that.

Because dude you are lucky that this particular situation is teaching you some good lesson out of it so better learn it now to get the better of it in the upcoming situation , you will face it with experience and with confident.

I am literally nothing , just a small dot of being existing in between this whole universe. Our problems are so small , compared to those who have the biggest of them doesn't get so complicated their suffocated mind like us.

Our inheritance is so acoustic that every time our minds are so ready to pre judge everything to the negative part of it's mindset rather than positive mindset which literally gives us feels.

There is room for me to improve , nor to have some co – operation from myself for actually performing well next time in whatever I try out thing in my life related to my cycle of mind.

I want to clear few things here , not everyone here actually be a winner on his own, nor they are winners all the time , nor winning all the time.

It's like the more you win , more pressure keeps adding on to you until it makes you so hyper tensed , keeps your expectations , frustrated that freaking you have to win.

It only makes your mind so childish , you actually forget what you have to do for keeping your tone highly active by day to day activity.

But,

If I keep on winning few times , losing many times it adds more calmness on me that losing is part, parcel of life.

So I actually concentrate on experiencing, embracing, embarking the journey than making some hasty decisions, awful thoughts about my life by not controlling my thoughts over someone's success story.

I may not be a life coach, mind reader for everyone who can actually tell you what you are thinking but "I" may be a good experienced life hacker for myself , many for myself which actually helped me accomplish some milestones with the same mindset.

So I feel that at least by applying some of these small real life examples you can actually achieve of whatever you are thinking that of dreaming it.

I believe strongly in the law of attraction which actually affirm your daily morning with it, you shall be granted by it only if you work toward it efficiently, loyally, with purest of heart only.

The amount of thoughts "I" have harvested till now has actually come into plantation process where all the efforts I have put on it has actually worked accordingly.

I am working so consistently on it that I am not worried at all how will it grow, does it give fruit

properly, to be frank I am not all thinking of the result "I" am only taking care of it without my self esteem , without expecting anything from it in return.
That's how I deal through whenever I see some problem arising to me , nor facing .
I just think of the process by nature for how it behaves accordingly to my behaviour so I can take rightful action in my life with rightful example so I won't be annoying myself or anyone in the progress of my life.
Trust me this second is very precious , every second the karma keeps hitting you back with the same behaviour of your very own applicability.
If someone is willing to listen to you completely by trusting in your life ideas , it gives them strong motto to build good bond, feelings, emotions with you.
Otherwise you will be just another person in their life rather than an 'Important person".
Think which option you would want to choose in those two, choice is yours, so does the outcome also hits you so badly.
Choose wisely.
Experience widely..!

CHAPTER FIVE

WHAT SHOULD 'U' DO!???

Basically if at all there is some relatable problems also in your life , "I" am going to recommend you to read further otherwise you can stop here , continue scrolling Instagram reels, stalk some unknown profile willingly or unwillingly.

If at all you are freaking concerned about your life at all, want some improvement , correction where it can actually shape you well into a appropriate shape in mind , heart .

Do continue , otherwise you can kindly close this book for good.

It's your wish totally , either to give a though from fresh perspective, perception so that it adds more value in your life than in my life.

See I am not saying that it would actually impact 100% in everyone's life, but definitely if applied from different scenarios, for implementing and adapting some behaviour of mine explained here.

'You' actually take everything for granted , including person in your life, problems to be faced/prevented,

situations will not be handled only when in simple proportion.
we actually start thinking only when it comes on our throat until then the time keeps ticking as if the clouds moving on daily basis.
Rather than actually enforcing , bracing ourselves rely too much on comfort zone, god, friends, family to solve our effect which is actually caused by us!.
What sin did they now create to come in your mess, actually see the non negotiable , non relevant to them than us.
You are invincible, limitless, unthankful for your own efforts of the emotions you have gone through by coming so far in your life is a big achievement until now.
you are not as inevitable for anyone to beat you. It's only you who can defeat you or make you win among yourself , first challenge always happens inside yourself & then with the outside world as opposition.
You are actually gifted with power of so self efficient positive energy to prove yourself worthy amongst yourself so no one can actually prove you that you are not even worthy of nothing.
Here is where you come into action by only trusting yourself by self faith , leap of hope by not backing yourself up when no one is actually responsible for your defeat or demotivation.
it's only you who is pulling yourself down , later on by others who is leading you all the way down to rock bottom.
You are actually more than beautiful than you think, from inside, outside , wholly , throughout just tell yourself , by affirming that you are the best & you can conquer the world.

You definitely will, all the time in this world is actually going in waste rather than give yourself some space for yourself by teaching , writing , or be accountable to the person who is good to you.

So all of your life goals planning never goes in vain, there is always a way to actually allow yourself to experience by all yourself.

This above way will be the best for all who are feeling that nothing is going in their way of life either in mental or physical act.

You know what in general , what all we think from everyone's perspective so that we shouldn't actually blame or give some difficulty to them by adjusting our instinctive, gut feeling.

What sense does it make for a being just to be all by themselves so it would get neutral result from all the approaches, outcomes.

Every , each one of person has a different struggle story from their childhood to now, it's not like we only grow through it on purpose.

You are gifted, enormously talented, fulfilled with all the basic organs, given good education, nutrition is provided accordingly, lifestyle is lived through , then what do you need?

Is it that you want God to gift you everything even not moving an inch from your bed , so you will only end up getting frustrated that you have not experienced anything in your life.

You think so negative that , our life is actually made up of up & downs literally right. Eventually you give up on it because things are actually not working out for the way you would want to go in it , mesmerize/ take everything in control.

Why you don't just sit in the last bench of life , take a test drive of the karma which automatically brings you lot of revenge, hatred, sweet memories, love , relation building in family.

By all the happy, sad, hasty , fickle, unstable decision we end up taking which it actually generalise it's own route for the success which we are eagerly waiting to celebrate.

CHAPTER SIX

HOW SHOULD YOU AND I ADAPT?

Firstly I must make up my soul , so even I end up being the most ill responsible for all the extinct bad behaviour, average efforts , minimal action taken forward.

Given aback at all for anyone to be precise , nor in any circumstance for everyone requires a basic qualification in either to enter into some field without their proper experience, so that obviously makes them demotivated at the end result.

So for whatever it might be you are trying always have some foundation ready for it , otherwise it will take such a downslide.

You will literally make a statement to whole world which is actually sleeping by their thoughts you feel nothing,of all them are observing you of what you are doing right by yourself, wrong by others.

Seriously life was so good in early life, with no tension, no expectaions , come the way life throws you

at, never be dull of the outcome of the process.
Every time it was like a learning experience & it would make us feel so excited too along with exploring new bunch of ideas of what to work , when.
But now there is very small room for the errors which we make, only perfection is required wherever you go.
they wouldn't appreciate you for your effort rather than that, degrade you of what a mess you have made out of it.
We all should find a purpose of our lives, it gives us that mental stability, exploration of thoughts, emotions, well being.
Otherwise there would be simply hell lot of complication.
Life at some point of time becomes very unpredictable for someone, some reason they have to retaliate nor realize for us.
It makes us think what else is left in our lives to actually by the mistakes/sins which we make everyday.
I am actually wondering in this lone forest which is quite dark one side, another side which is actually very dark where I can't see anything but yet there happens to be the brightest sunrise, sunset.
Well it happens to be coincidence right along with darkest side has the brightest of the sun rising and setting, that's life guys who have all the opportunities filled with.
always will be having a baggage of problems which would be very difficult to carry all through their life , with this some give up on themselves , on their goals which actually makes them think they are overrated/ assumptions which actually leads to negativity.

Hence it's proved right the more you want to do good for the society but the inner monster from them controls us from being that successful/exceptional who does all the hard work with lots of efforts from a direction.

perhaps these small amount of ants which actually can't control us behave in a way & make us think we are the ones who are behaving wrong in the society.

Well yes, goddammit it's always us who will have to get adjust to others feelings, roadmap of future which would be total opposite side of the map which we actually will be dreaming off from a long time.

you know this villain of everyone's timeline is this bloody situation , which henceforth comes from this silly word called expectation that everyone should always do right by me , the way I did right.

But in life always we should be a giver rather than a receiver , there lies the satisfaction for a human being so generous in this time being is very rare.

Right now everyone is so eternally misjudging about their own identity, self established due to the out sources denying that we are actually not fit for the appropriate work which actually will be even dreaming in our sleep since childhood.

in reality we are someone else who is actually hiding from our true reflection of the mirror which is showing us that it is not us, but "It's all about sacrificing right"?

I start regretting , o why didn't I take up the risk when I had a chance to make it right by myself , for my well being.

It's all written in our destiny we say right , but atleast have we ever tried to change the fate which is written?

I have tried so many times, be so confusing for myself. For my own being I only want to happen on my

own will.
I don't want someone's influence, inspiration to affect my life cycle. It's said you have your own karma , problems, pros, discomfort , means, cause, process of actually applying or implementing in their own individual lives.
I can say it all depends on their smart work, essence of life how much they want in their life accordingly should be put otherwise it would be a waste of time cooking so much of knowledge which is actually not even worth of brain storming to the children or to anyone to be precise.
It's very simple for a failed individual in the exam of life , to actually have a breather from everything that has made him downfall so they will realise whatever the procedure which made them believe that the result will be in their favour.
Since there are people in this universe who are actually way more stronger, have more connections , more richer, but who am I?
I am just an ordinary being, who would want to grow into a meaningful, essential , trustful, lust less , eventful , fruitful , sufficient less , human who will actually tells /explains without any self esteem to every individual to my circle possible who crosses the path with me , see what would I get from all this.
A satisfaction which is worth of enormous of wealth , which gives me so much of motivation, inspiration, eventful of memories for me to be actually grateful in this small period of time which god has given us with beautiful tiny planet of existence.
Yet we still fight so much for our ego, religion, race, accustomed behaviour, property, attitude, feelings,

emotions, love, land, politics, unity, prosperity, peace.
I am just a temporary/tiny being , in this huge
universe where my existence doesn't have a guarantee
or warranty as a product which we actually order from a
store or an online marketplace.
even above all this we all forget try to be some fake
person for the sake of the person whom will be pushing
us to be like a puppet, which would make us so
emotionally like robot without any feeling (literally like
an automation which would be data fed to us , to behave
accordingly without any of our freedom by choice).
Why there is no choice given to us, nor any
differentiate denied so that the mental space of every
living being can actually have that clarity of whatever is
doing right by their side than their choice..
The lifecycle of a human being actually evolves
around like a cycle , which benefices from starting as
child into the world transforms evolves from taking care
us the parents love.
We get loved, attention, acknowledged, astonished
for the behaviour of response we get from everyone we
cross the paths or front of them.
Once we come off from a age , turn into a elderly
citizen we become more smaller baby whom would ,
should be taken care of but the most important part
here is there would be no interest for anyone to take
care of perhaps it would bring more of irritation for one
being to taken care by.
I hereby tell , there isn't any one person nor one
being to prove some behaviour, it is all about bringing
the equality of humanity for circle to actually enhance ,
provide all the living in one circle.

Sincerely it seems like our work, duty to give all the insights for someone in their life but for our concern they are least concerned about opinion we give towards their life above that also impacts a lot.

perhaps what would it give for a being to just put information about themselves , also brings realisation for them hence it would be like a reminder in an individual life.

Even though the distance to be travelled for a sincere request of a accordance goal which will be required sacrifice , given that time in the process of effective existence.

What satisfaction it shall bring for an independent survivor who is willing to achieve something from that victory , it shall only bring short term pleasure , satisfaction but that calmness only appears from within by enhancing /bracing ourselves to be more stronger in emotional way or in the losing state of mind.

It explains us how big the state of the matter is our universe here , you can always comeback stronger than yourself by competing against your own will which is more evil than the monkey present in us.

CHAPTER SEVEN

WHY DO WE KEEP ON RUNNING FROM EVERYTHING WHICH LIFE ACTUALLY GIFTS US WITH ?

The value of it's existence would be only known when the warranty of that living actually makes us regret by fading/moving away from as usual way which would literally tear us apart into small pieces , lifelong we still will be collecting all that tiny particles so called memories to inhabit our daily activities, just so to push our ability , capabilities.

Why shouldn't we value which is actually in front of us , accept it and go ahead with the journey according to the way which leads the way, instead we actually give up on our loyalty.

Go in search for short time results which never really helps us in any way rather only give negative vibes as usual , it is very simple to get attached and detached from a person/ thing.

In the process you will actually learn lot of nature's errors , destiny play game , choices over priorities , regrets on decisions , loosing focus on long term goals, sacrificing over commitments, importance giving on toxic behaviour / people.

CHAPTER EIGHT

WHY ME?

Is this battle in myself, why it is so active making me giving lots of negative thoughts. It's actually killing my peace of mind which was resting a while ago but now it is up & running due to the comparison of the abilities present in my competition.
While I have to accept that my thinking, performance , ability to behave under pressure , to keep on working until a end result which makes me feel hell yeah , I'm better than yesterday of me!!.
Why do you consider so less of yourself, since there are worst than the way you are. Tell yourself you are the best in the world, affirmation and the law of attraction is very mandatory for once being in today's world.
Obviously due to the increasing population, competition.
All you got to do is only know your strengths , keep improving it regularly so you will be the best of yourself.
Master of yourself, Slave of none..
Hence if you start implementing this in your daily life routine , even your weakness shall be your best friend.
Never be a loser , rather be a slayer of your own thoughts because nevertheless The battle of life can only

be fought by you and yourself only.
Never rely on someone, so it is slavery because you
are giving your strength to them . You will be only
listener than the giver.
If I am the known person of myself then all my
secrets , strength , power, peace, weakness, negativity
will be all transformed into a whole new line with
positives and negatives in accordance to the equality of
you.
It all comes under only one chance of question, your
gut/instinct feeling for you to observe to change and
embrace our soul into the process for the progress in the
life.
I am always expecting something or someone to help
me out from any small or big the problem /difficulty.
Why wouldn't you actually see the full picture ?
The whole essence of life is here to keep us upgrading
with learning of new skills, difficulties.
Always be a problem solver not be a problem giver.
Period.
The internal problem of an successful individual will
always be that he/she will be more selfish, self
-obsessed, self – attached so they would be well settled
in individual lives , perhaps for us it would be like a
mountain to climb for all those abilities.
More than that we are more empathized,
sympathized persons than those of successful
millionaires who only care about their happiness than
the whole world of laughter.
The merer we get involved in someone else's mess
until it get cleared we shall also be stuck there in the life
journey than it's better for us to mind our own mess, it's
very clear for one to be atleast in their own journey.

The less distracted/detached you are from any closest person which you wish that want to be a part of it , there your downfall starts .
Why would anyone give you the recipe of success , even though you get after lots of asking from anyone of your circle but it's not of no use.
It's actually been applied in his/her own dish for making a delicious meal so it shall not all apply in your life, because you have got different taste of meal which you want to create.
Yeah it requires own efforts , not any shortcut will take you the closing line of the endline for the result to be victory.
Life is very delicate just like the tip of the ice cream , so will have to go through it very smoothly otherwise if you make hurry and take hasty decisions all the cream would fall off , so it will be obviously frustrating to eat only the cone.

WHAT IF I TELL YOU THAT YOU CAN ACTUALLY TURN YOUR PAIN INTO A POSITIVE OUTCOME/ ENERGY!!!

Yes it is very easy for one to turn their negative mindset/feeling/emotion into a very emotional journey of positive set of outcomes travelling through different timelines of the search for an answer by their existence.

Why we actually embrace for one being so in active for the outbreak that we have caused all the wrongdoing in our lives and blame it on the typical situation so we cannot carry that guilt lifelong on us , but what mistake has the situation done for you by covering all the regrets that you have undergone by all alone by yourself.

For one to be so playing the blame game on every single small he/she taken, then obviously you will be circling all around the problem each and every time you try to overcome , you would have committed an other crime of blaming.

There will be no growth at all in your life if at all this would be so constant throughout.

The only solution for this to acceptance for whatever you have done until now, making sure you are not repeating the same old mistake again , again but in a new way until the universe make you realise that you are wrong doing , the circle will be evolving.

Until , unless you feel that you have done enough damage to your energy , timeline for a certain outcome with conscious effort from the truth.

Rather than you waiting for a miracle in your life by making that false acquisition that destiny has actually something written over my head for to happen, trust me it's bullshit!.

Always be the one who creates miracle, never wait for the destiny to happen. Make it fall into its place of whatever wish you would want to happen in this world to wish for.

It would be a fool for anyone to be just waiting , wasting time than you know go for the opposite side of mind which is actually making you more weak, scared of. There lies the answer for your question of winning through anything, anyone in life...

The art of sub conscious should be so pure that even in dreams it will be activating the most favourite person, situation which you would want that to turn into a reality than to keep just as a dream.

If at all there would be no better persons than the other in your life, would you be running behind them without the important part of life which actually tells us

the importance of being loyal to the few persons/
individual who at all want to take a important decision
would approach you no matter what the situation.
It's not at all about not having time. It's about making
time.
The greatest of the individuals will always have a
downfall , so never keep on fluctuating your value of
interest on the ones who keeps on winning.
The more you fall , greater height you will reach.
Better be on a team who is losing consistently, they
will eventually see a success with the victory of the
margins which is inevitable.
Remember we always think , the process of
champions would be so great and will have to follow the
same procedure for being a champion.
The secret for being a champion is to consistency,
persistence on the top priority m perception over the
best probability.
It's probably none of my business to actually tell all
these tricks but still you know always the most
experienced one would be who has lost too many battles
yet so far , little more away from the line of margin by a
small error.
Even thoroughly it's not self efficient to behave also
so perfect all the time, always try to strike the balance in
between both between your conscious and sub state of
conscious mind.
Then only you can empower, overcome the ordinary
not just by defeating it rather than breaking your own
old self even with your intentions being so right with the
first go itself.
It is said always find the solace before you start
encroaching a specific target of goals , dreams which

you want to overcome from your futuristic life than your present one, so what is actually holding you back.
Just go with the flow, planned , prepared , questionnaire in your mind over the probabilities you shall face, possibilities you would get at the end, priorities over the choice of people / work you shall choose by choice than chance.
I am a fighter who just never wants to give up on persons/things which I intended to force or insist myself that it would be possible.
One day if I keep on showing up to the opponent which is myself but how does it often make me realise that the motivation doesn't come from some videos, speech nor by a person telling you to do it perhaps it's a inner feeling which comes naturally within.
Rather than exaggerating about things of how to execute them eventually it is by which intention you apply yourself in the given situation , otherwise it would have been a different scenario all together.

CHAPTER TEN

WHY ARE WE ALWAYS PUSHED TOWARDS THE WRONG SIDE OF THE WIND, DIRECTION BY THE NATURE ?

It is to swim in the strongest of the forces against the negative side of the environment, so we can actually see the overall impact of one's ability, capability , availability of discomfort provided in the process.
We are the warriors of the future by telling all the possible, even worst outcomes so we would be good to acknowledge the better result otherwise it shall actually demotivate us by putting so down with all the stress,

mental illness which becomes stronger and meaner.

The more inevitable I or perhaps us try to inculcate in our one's experience from the daily experience of thoughts will be also be so relatable in any given scenario.

I am no a good actor myself nor who can actually enact as one in front for anyone but it would be not my form of act to complain anything about someone to them, it goes totally opposite in nature.

Perhaps in anywhere where you go the prosperity , peace , environment , adaptability , presence of mind , common sense nobody teaches us how to inculcate in our daily life.

This miscomputation keeps on occurring all the time until we get to a point where nobody is actually required to change your mind, approach towards any decision you make.

From morning 5 AM through the sunrise start getting ready for the day ahead, plan it accordingly .

But in between that chaos we all forget. It's not in the best we can actually try and enact perfect all the time.

Always in life we shall have an alternative excuse of not doing whatever we would have wanted to do , just think the exact side of it . Definitely you will end up doing the wanted but the unwanted from the mind perspective.

It's a win , win situation for you .

What we sense , Oh shit there is someone actually watching us on our present behaviour. How would someone actually respond after I get failed in whatever the process I had attempted for!!.

Why are we scared by others , when we know the actual sense of our body, sense, hard work, time , energy

that you have put in hasn't gone in vain at all.
This definitely shall be a comedy of error if we start
behaving according to the situation , result coming in
our way of life.
Our life is just as the food we order to the waiter,
We only get what we order,
Rest all mustn't be preferred,
The first time when we get an opportunity in life
must be seized, same as when waiter delivers the starter
to us.
'Opportunities doesn't come twice knocking.'
While riding /driving "never complain" by honking,
rather accept on and find a different way to go,
In life too never ever blame on others, put all your
problems only on your shoulders and carry on, perhaps
than that no one helped me.
We never tell all the truth to everyone nor to 'the
closed ones' in our life, rather tell it in our perspective to
defend ourselves.!
The more you start caring about what others think,
the more you start getting weak.
The closer you stay, the painful it gets,
More far you stay, the closer you become
If you are not doing it now, you are never doing it
later.
Life is a journey, not a destination.
It only matters how you travel and not where to
We may be the masters of our thoughts, but we are
not slaves to our emotions.
Sometimes when we find love, we push it away or
choose to ignore it.
No matter who you are, no matter what you did, no
matter where you have come from, you can always

"change".
A lot of drama could be avoided if more people just
learned how to not react.

CHAPTER ELEVEN

IN THIS FAKE WORLD WHO ARE REALLY YOUR REAL ONES!!??.

Take a day off and just think to yourself.
Think what you have done to them.
Think what they have done to you back, learn now
and never do the mistake again of just being there for
them but they not being by your side.
Think who actually stays by your side, who actually
cares for you.
All by yourself.
And don't ever push away your loved ones just like
that..
Because one day it will kill you from inside and it will
make you so fake that you will live very happily with
your friends, everyone, but deep inside you know how
much they(your loved ones) loved you.

If you avoid them it's okay, they will stay by your side no matter what but the ones whom you are with who are so fake but feels real to you.

But

One day later any problems comes those friends or anyone who you thought will be by your side in your difficult times, don't even think it in your dreams that they will stay by your side in your difficult times they will just pass on like clouds.

So the true ones the ones who loves you truly will stay the end of your breath with you, next to you, they just don't care loosing to you but they would never want to loose you so..

Blurred past evaporating from teardrops. Unending dreams carving an arc of smile. And a fleeting life, negotiating between the two...."

Just be clear as these clouds are, even if they hide their secret in the clouds they don't hide it longer, they shower it down in the form of rain.

In a life full of metro rides, there are aged couple, lovers, colourful girls, young and handsome boys with their breakup mindset, YA according to us we are handsome, aged women's, best friends of both gender, family, the people who we travel with in metro is so peaceful and amazing, y can't we continue to live like that even in our daily lives?.

Rains wash away all the dirt, but the words which are told by closed ones never wash our pain out till the end.

Feelings!

When we are born and brought up by our parents the feelings will be over our parents only, the people we look around often.

We tend to cry if we see strangers, if we are surrounded by the persons whom we see regularly we tend to be happy.
As we grow up our feelings goes to our friends, the girls we like, we forget to have feelings on our parents, as we will be grown up we will have a gf/bf where we give full importance, time, feelings to them rather we neglect parents, family, friends.

Feelings will be over our loved ones only .
And at last If they leave you very badly where (you have pushed away your family, friends, parents and given importance for your loved ones, there is no one now to support you when they leave you from your life.)
My conclusion (I'm not saying you to love, love but don't avoid your family, friends, parents, keep it normal for everyone, give importance to everyone).
So that even if your loved ones dump you (You will be having your friends, family, parents to support you).
People drive their own car,(life) in their own way(living their life),at one point of time they will stop obvious bcz they will get to know they are heading in wrong direction.
So don't tell them that your route is wrong if u tell them they will go more faster so let them reach that destination (situation) after that they will only head towards correct direction.
We give way for ambulance, without knowing who is there inside like that in our lives if we don't disturb or spoil other lives there will be no problem in our daily life.
The evolution of life is slowly developing lot of intolerance attitude which is quite not acceptable in the

society nor for the well being , it demands everyone to be so irresponsible of what irrespective consequences.

Why are we like this in today's world only focused on ourselves only , why we don't actually try to adapt some giving attitude for them who are willing to try and give their 200% in their efforts of making our life better.

It all matters of a small piece of kindness, graciousness, enlightenment , awareness for an individual to actually make someone better than them in life , so the life gets more challenging in order to acknowledge and encash their goal.

Otherwise what rush will be there on top of the hill if we climb alone , never get to share the experience along the way of how each other fell, how much difficulty got to face, milestones conceded all along , whilst the nature admiration explanation will actually be missed and so difficult to enhance the environment.

So if we make a conscious effort of bringing along more , more people in our circle of life . It gets more interesting , challenging , overwhelming throughout the process so we can endure all our pain , misery , mystery , success , motivation , inspiration to one another.

Otherwise it shall be so depressing/ demotivating when we start travelling all along the journey , only in the starting you feel so free and independent but once you actually get bored of all the things doing again & again. Obviously there shall be no support or to push you few times where you lack to tell get up from your laziness.

Humans always want to be in centre of people , whether they are known pr unknown , we always want to get listened to , we must be heard , we crave for attention sometimes, as the loneliness bring lots of lost wounds which shall make you dive deep into the agony of life so you wouldn't want to get up again.

It intensifies our subconsciousness to behave like that many times but as I said earlier always try to replicate the alternative course of mind , so we can achieve what we want to do than the monkey mind in there.

The more we try to restrict that monkey mind, it grows stronger and stronger that it will actually implement , plant whatever the monkey mind trying to think the alternative thing.

CHAPTER TWELVE

SO HOW SHOULD I MAKE A CONSCIOUS EFFORT OF AFFIRMING WHAT I WANT TO ACHIEVE THAN THAT OF MIND?

The only secret here is to implanting your monkey mind , order it to that you are doing correct , make me remember so that I will do it again so my dopamine shall get its effect.

If we try to tell like this , obviously it will reflect in a opposite way.

So there is one more way , you can actually order your conscious mind that you will gift something which is very special of what it needs of craving for artificial things. In order for it only if you follow my instructions, put up a sticky notes saying all the dates of a calendar and keep on cancelling all the dates whenever it promptly achieves the day.

At the end of two months /three whenever your specific target ends gift your conscious mind so it will keep on defending your subconscious & monkey mind in there which is thinking that it is stronger than us.

Let us make a fool out of it , so we get whatever we are actually keeping in touch of conscious effort.

In these given ways , there is another way for whom they think it is not working.

It is to practice yoga , meditation for everyday in their life so they can actually give direction to the thoughts so the above examples would never required them to make.

But yeah it takes time for a being to practice yoga and meditation for keeping consistent , continuous.

So it is a long term , it takes long term of days/ months to get actually practice it with but will give a lifelong worth full of whatever affirmations which you want to achieve in your life.

Am I in a hurry to actually get everything instantly , constantly everything in my life so everyone in my life should actually get disappeared then and there without my consent right. Then only I will have that freedom of heights to achieve whatever I can enjoy throughout my life.

I will give a small example, think that only you are living in this whole world and don't have any one single human all over the world because you actually wished for it, it was granted.
The rest remained the same , all the food , nature , cars , flights , all the artificial things.
For how many days , months will you be actually happy or satisfactory , enjoy all the superficial excitement throughout.
You would crave for someone who actually love/like them atleast after your dopamine effect actually gets disappeared/dismantled from your life.
So if you wish for someone who you actually care for, then that person wishes for the person they wish for and the process goes on until it becomes full universe yet again.
The calmness over the chaos when you visit a place, restaurant , trip , or wherever you go .
All the time your mind asks for a company to be around so you actually don't be a lone soul otherwise why would we feel happy when we go through someone over the journey!!
So tell me , it doesn't make a difference right or it does right literally!
Why don't we act so cruelly that nothing is in our hands all the time, when there is so much power of to make everything right by your way of receiving all the love , light , pain from anyone who you actually fear from failure..
It all takes some time for an individual to behave appropriate , it is about making time for someone who is actually quite special than anyone , rather than telling I don't have time.

Well it all takes over the priority over someone which you feel from intolerance of the subconsciousness that whenever it doesn't feel right , as it fades away just like that without any reason at all.

So decide to yourself where you actually want to belong to the group of achievers nor to the ones of selfish ones.

The capability of any living being is so delicate, so try to be nice whomever you cross the paths by.

You never know when the karma actually hits you very hard for any given reason , there shall not be an explanation from god himself for actually you experiencing or going through.

The examples of intolerance always makes you feel so empowered , dethrone also few times but it is always going in two direction.

So be nice to the nature, humans, things to manage all the extreme law of attraction by negative thought which you actually manifest always gets in the situation which would want to make it for real in reality of errors , make you start worry over the issues which you had never thought of.

I always want a comfort zone to behave so that I have actually achieved so much in my life, done enough activities, created lots of opportunities to others, donated a lot to orphanage that I shall take rest/nap all over my day just to pass the time and get over the day , get on to the night so I can sleep more.

Why will I actually confess to myself that I have done enough for to actually be resting so much all along , the greats never take rest nor nap in the day , never pass the time to actually come over the night and behave I have successfully wasted one precious day of mine right?

So you know that's why I always try to behave so
much out of motive that there is no satisfactory thing in
this world, it is not so small to conquer everything &
everyone at one point of time.
It is very possible for anyone to be brutally honest
with them so that we don't get over confident by
boasting that we start degrading some person who is
actually quite famous in this field of work than to get
some positives of how they got there perhaps than to
retaliate by comparing to someone who is better.
The beauty of willingness to do the same thing of
approaching the same habit of the process will bring lot
of negative energy to you , than inculcating new habits
so that no one has actually explored.
I shall have smooth journey than merely ups and
downs in my life .
It all depends on how you actually convince yourself
no matter what , I will go through this unexplored way
than moving slowly in a traffic way which is going very
dramatic.
Always take a break from reality or from whatever
you are trying to achieve so the conscious mind gets so
much of oxygen to breathe along difficult situations
ahead , rather than forcing it to push it's more than the
energy.
I intend to show the nature , so any activity which
actually excites it as any movie, songs, fancy restaurant.
The activity also gets interesting, you get more ideas ,
solutions to actually make your intentions pretty much
clear about the thoughts, intriguing all the way long to
establish it on your mind.
Otherwise the void shall will slowly start to form
which shall make shallow deep effect or the inactive way

of achieving the most of all thing.

CHAPTER THIRTEEN

WHY IS IT SO IMPORTANT TO HAVE A BREAK FROM THE DAILY RACE OF LIFE ?

The steps that we take all life will be actually tired taking all the stress, inevitable of load.

The moment you give a break from everything strongly desire to achieve in one day, than it actually starts to breathe that nothing is going to be achievable for me.

It finds its peace, calmness, core strength of our thoughts, affirmations slowly start to grow more effectively in order to take it slow as per day.

The confidence in us starts to boost itself , greets us by saying thank you for giving me this break. As it feels like a lifelong to actually make peace with me in the ahead journey.

So in accordance to make ourselves , I am making
more hasty decisions so that I will be questioned by
myself again that why didn't I listen to myself.
I don't know how to actually elaborate enormous in
it's own way or in an alternate source.
The result in which intentions also approaches us by
many other elements.
In order to perceive some or the other many
perception of our strong positive feelings , perseverance
to actually hold on to whatever affirmations in our
manifesting thoughts to achieve in our lives.
The priorities we set all over just the way we get
treated , the way how one actually puts in the amount of
efforts , the positive vibes one actually share with us all
along , the possible affect ensures that whom shall be
remained among.
In any other's lives nor some other being always
make sure that the true self making a apt for ourselves
rather than you yourself.

CHAPTER FOURTEEN

I AM YOU

If people are trying to bring you down,
it usually means you are above them.
Most times when someone is trying to sabotage what
you have going for you, they think of you as a threat.
LIFE IS MADE OF UPS AND DOWNS. WHEN IT
GOES UP, ENJOY THE RIDE, BECAUSE IT WILL GO
DOWN SOON AND WHEN IT GOES DOWN, STAY
POSITIVE, BECAUSE IT WILL GO UP AGAIN.
YOU WILL FIND YOUR WAY
Even if you find yourself
struggling to make a way
out of these uncertain days,
remember you are strong and brave,
you are still capable of doing your best.
Some days the pain will be too deep
and the only answer you will have
is carrying on anyway.
But you will be okay,
Despite it all my friend,
you will find your way.
I genuinely fell for someone when I wasn't
searching for love, I was searching for peace.

I was searching for myself and found a friend
who became the love of my life
.
Sometimes you need to focus on growing yourself and
you'll run into what's destined for you.
"I hope that in the end you'll be satisfied. Not only
satisfied, but happy.
I hope you'll tell me you gave
your best and on days you couldn't, you allowed
yourself to rest without feeling guilty about it.
I hope you found love at some point, that you
cherished it and did not take it for granted.
And when it crashed and burned and you held the
shattered pieces in your bloody palms, I hope you
could at least learn something about yourself.
You
grew from the things that broke you. I'm so proud
of you for staying soft in a world that tries to
harden your heart every day.
I hope that at the end of your days you will not
regret anything you did and didn't do. I want to
hear you say "I made mistakes and I fucked up, but
I lived. I lived through it all and looking back, I
would not change a single thing."'
—/
Note to self:
Better days are coming your way.
(Taken from my Blog)

Who the f... Is I? Am!

I who is becoming more aware of the reality to
become fearless of overcoming failures of regular
intervals,
Am just being ambitious, ambivert sometimes,
extrovert many times in approaching problems of people
and mine.
Rarely I turn into an introvert just to realise or to
regret of the situation.
Am I behaving in multiple faces just as one which is
very predominant settled towards the society.
One which is myself who is hiding inside me but will
only come out when no one is around whom you
wouldn't want to share it with them.
What's the use of simply sitting at one place and
deciding upon another person whether he/she is a
monster or not.
Perhaps we ourselves don't know who and what
cause we can bring through to effect and immediately
affect other's life.
Let's better start controlling our actions into one
direction rather than changing into multiple single lane
roads better than one single highway of six lane.
Life's a secretive game, you don't know when you will
be brought in to play what kind of role which you are not
aware of.
It does not matter with whom you entry but with
whom you execute the plan.
Bonding differs from person to person depends on
how you calculate their intervein towards your
individuality

CHAPTER FIFTEEN

WHO IS AN I?

In some terms I can be very selfish, many times confident, and true to himself/herself, helping the ones who are actually facing too many issues in their current scenario through their epic journey of failures.

Since my childhood whenever I started to keep my feet down was struggling hell-bent, I was scared that I would fall down badly & hurt myself badly; eventually.

I did fall down many times, and in the process got up on my own or with the support of another individual so I can manage myself with whatever uncertain consequences, in the end, I will be facing.

So whilst I was going through this process, the conscious mind was actually without my consent to behave in a certain manner which was a shocker even for my sub-conscious mind which never understood me myself.

It is a natural thing that every child goes through but in between all that events of trying over & over wasn't that difficult or demotivating at all ever since I eventually stood up finally one day as the strongest child ever!!

The intent in which I got to learn the amateur/easy/difficult level doesn't really matter to me more than the outcome of how slowly grasping all the muscle memory, failing many more times than feeling happy over the procedure.

Always love your own perception of how you are actually going to come to the closest point in your life so it actually takes you to places where you wouldn't even think of your capability, positiveness, and perseverance all from my ability to achieve.

I will have to start inculcating having more or less strength to encash all the adaptability so no one can actually make you feel bad about yourself, start comparing yourself to them.

Start to offend, degrading yourself which shall bring lots of toxic behavior in us to satisfy our dopamine and make ourselves that of what we had thought in our low.

How to be more self-satisfied with yourself, given talents will share a story with you.

Character names in the story;

Arohan who is the protagonist will be actually facing difficulties in his life as casual in common but how he comes out from that, inculcating the abilities and character growth shall be explained in brief in this so you can also implement it in your lives.

Sanidhya is an outrageous, extrovert, tolerating the inheritance that she actually overcame in her early stage of life which made her so excited, and interested for everyone to actually get in her life just to duplicate her experience in their lives.

Arohan was a very much introvert back in his childhood school days , as he still was having that crush for his classmate Sanidhya.

But as he was scared talking to her, seeing her rather preferred to still follow her behind with a gap of 800 meters, even though she was not turning back and seeing him but he was amused and thrilled just to take the same steps as she followed.

Arohan didn't take the courage or the opportunities which came earlier to him many times.

He had best friend named Manasa who was pretty much close to him in talking sense into him, giving suggestions to him on how to talk to

Sanidhya in the right approach but for Manasa Sanidhya was just a normal friend as they wouldn't hang out much nor talk to each other well as Arohan used to do.

Arohan actually told Manasa that he wants to confess his love to Sanidhya , so Manasa fills in some reality that your existence doesn't even matter for her because she has no idea about you

She first told to talk to her directly make some good memories together later we shall think about asking out.

As Arohan was actually not willing to take the risk and talking to her , all he could do is follow her and just to see her happy with her zone and friends.

Later I went through a very deep thought that , for me even though if I start getting to know her coming into the zone of her existence there would be obviously too much of competition for him.

I decided that I will definitely look over her in my future rather than waste my time on love.

After 12 years

As I started to grow elderly, at the age of 24 will be having own cafe with restobars.

Arohan will be very much settled in his life with good income from his startup's but for his luck covid struck and the happy part still Manasa was her best friend, she created a WhatsApp school group, and life takes a u-turn for him with Manasa following Sanidhya to Arohan was really excited to see and his face was glowing to see she was single

So Arohan with all his prayers and luck , Sanidhya accepted his Instagram request and started to follow back, rest was history re written for him in golden words.

Arohan with all his guts confessed to Sanidhya that he is still having a crush on Sanidhya since childhood.

As she had just come out of a very toxic relationship for many years, she was feeling happy with all the things going on with Arohan and didn't know that this guy was actually following her from school.

Arohan surprised Sanidhya by asking her out for a date with his knees touching the ground, one pointing towards her holding her single hand, she was in tears and just hugged him with tears

kissing him with the feelings of emotions running through both their veins.

That day and night he called Manasa to tell about this date which she doesn't know but as he kept calling her phone was switched off.

I called her mother later he got to know that they are in burial ground at the night of their beautiful night had to see her best friend funeral, that broke him into tears .

So as Arohan was not feeling anything without his energy, emotions running blank.

Sanidhya held his hand and took somewhere far away from all this , where there was only fogg as they only could sense their breath to each other perhaps than their bodies was unaware and unravelling itself from everything which happened today.

Sanidhya couldn't resist his presence which was full of pain, agony gave him a tight hug and she was going to kiss him to get him back alive and running.

They both her a loud voice from the background that Manasa was shouting arohannnnn .. My dad body is missing ....

As these three went near the burial ground there was no one , even the relatives weren't there at that place , as suddenly it turned into a beautiful park, everyone were amazed from it.

How many more times they tried to come over the park around, they would end at that same spot until after a few hours of testing they found a elderly person riding bicycle calling out , funeral ... funeral 10 rupees only .

As these 3 tried to call out him to reach him, even asked him lift but the latter didn't respond, so their last option they stood in front of him as he went through them.

As every minute was passing by , the shade of that elderly person was fading away.

Later they got to know it was manasa father who was riding bicycle as a soul in the transitional world /Middle world .

When Arohan called out Ravichandran uncle what is this and what's happening to us and what are you doing?

Ravichandran Uncle told the previous story of how , Sanidhya ex had kidnapped him and hit him to the death because of that I was stuck in this in between works as my wishes and dreams were left incomplete!!!!

Just because of you Arohan I'm stuck here and you are the key to me going back to earth and even for your crush and my daughter.

As Sanidhya and Manasa were unaware of it as they couldn't see Ravichandran's uncle!

I can narrate so much more insights into this, but I want you guys to actually take over from here.

I shall be delivering justice for my readers perhaps it would add some task for you to actually read through the book to find out the answer which we actually always crave/expect from everything.

I shall be incomplete without it right, feeling inwards regarding some or the other thing actually impacts us that whatever is going through in our lives will be extinct one day.

CHAPTER SIXTEEN

THE FIGHT BETWEEN ALL THE CATEGORIES;

Over any living/artificial things which we shall quarrel for the copyright, what difference does it make when everyone is actually working with one intention for the result orientation from whatever expectation/ satisfaction it brings in our daily lives right?

The intolerance from others can actually grow in their life than you, we are just being selfish in our own ways just to be successful & get recognized among rest of all.

The incapability of handling all the issues in our lives actually goes all out on us, not just by our intentions but also by egoistic feelings over toxic behavior, and arrogant responses in some issues related to just human things.

I intended to actually give up on few things in my life which actually never worked my way around for quite some long time , for my surprise it made sense for me to realise as an individual ; there is not one being in the universe to taste success / nor whatever to be actually in his plate of life.

The amount of right confidence , struggle for actually making it worth right through our efforts which will prove others wrong , especially even our own self shall be in shock.

I can openly tell to all the beings out there ; In this world nobody has a perfect love-story which actually starts with lots of butterflies in our stomach.

Excitement in sharing the numbers, hyped over sharing all the topics which you always dreamt of doing since the time you were given a thought of it.

Previous bad experiences which made you feel bad about yourself from you got criticised for just being good in the relationship, understanding one which actually steps in our lives we become so independent from our own perspective that it makes us automatically right in whatever matter situation we are in.

The more time I start to judge some or the other qualities in our lives who wouldn't have seen any other face of ours to co – exist , but rather than actually taking them out of the equation makes them even stronger than before.

Power of acceptance is powerful in any relationship whether it be in love , in marriage .

Only when you actually make the bond between you guys win, typically to be said relationship to be formed takes lot of patience, time , efforts , compromises, sacrifices , breakage of ego /attitude also.

If I don't actually have good intentions before starting the conversation of whatever end – result

which you will be looking forward doesn't happen overnight instantly ;
For it eventually you must had the blessings of god himself by being in that zone far from all the toxic friends nor any individual who is forcing/ fluctuating your mind.
The tagline which everyone tells us 'Marriages are made in heaven'??
How is it even related to that of the quote but seriously I can answer it but not completely ,evidently.
I shall atleast come close to it , where the meaning of it actually makes you think of why not getting all that extra attention from anyone than from my family!!
It is happy to actually have one , along with that has that much only chaos in it.
Involvement is actually like giving all the credit to the sub state of mind which is inculcated rightfully to implement in specifically individuals who actually intended to act wholesomely appropriate , accurate all the time even when they are right or wrong it doesn't make a difference to them.
In our lives as we try to ensure more of calculative risk management skills , less by the side of ending in losing side, expected to be cared / nurtured;
I assure that even though the time period of few/ many people in this life have actually gone good into worse, worse to worser , best to better , nothing to something more to of a great height
Due to some that small initial movement from where their luck which they achieve it but the years long sacrifice , smart work comes into existence & makes a difference between rest of them than you.

Intellectual facts/truths about the reality of life cannot be shared with everyone so that they can be aware of them all the time.

In fact, the hardest of the results come off from the smoothest of approaches even though we have enough power to go through the pain of failure/society.

Why is there always in our lives who intends to interfere in our private life just to create some unneeded measures or irrelated problems?

So we can get disturbed all the time even with most of them shall be so toxic that no one does the mistake nor the trust issues all over throughout!!

If you sob out of happiness, the first tear will come from the right eye, but if you cry out of sorrow, it will come from the left.

Food prepared by someone else tastes much better than your own preparation, even when you use the same recipe.

Hearing a single negative thing could damage a minimum of five positive memories.

Being alone is harder for your health than you really believe.

We're the most imaginative in the night and the least creative in the day.

Being home alone and isolated for a long time is just as bad for your well-being as smoking 15 cigarettes a day.

People are more likely to blame someone in the case when something negative happens.

Studies also found that people who are in a position of influence and power are very poor in determining other people's emotions.

The force of authority may have the same effect on a
human as a traumatic brain injury.
People read quicker with longer lines but prefer
shorter lines.
Larger groups make worse and more subjective
choices than smaller groups of people.
If you can't interrupt the stream of thinking at night,
write it down.
This is going to put your mind at ease so that you can
relax.
Women have half as many pain receptors on their
bodies as males, but they have a much greater threshold
for pain.
Physically, repetition affects the brain as new
associations are made between brain cells.
The maximum number of close relationships/
friendships you can maintain is between 50 and 150.
Your brain is doing more imaginative work when
you're sleepy.
It is also found that staying optimistic about the
future can powerfully shield people from physical and
mental illness.
Seeing others favourably shows our positive
characteristics, seeing others negatively reveals our
negative attributes.
Depression is often referred to as the product of
thought. Imagination causes issues that didn't exist.
Being happy around people makes you happier.
Convincing yourself that you slept well tricks your
brain into believing you did.
The sort of music you listen to influences the way you
view the world.

The utmost reaction for one, almost everyone will be just receiving the answers from within than listening to the outside world for it.

Why the inner other self of monkey mindset by chance will never be able to satisfy even if you give whatever the world it asks for!

A goal without some hard facts unknown without your victory to chase it all around in its hemisphere at all.

The challenges and problems faced by the individual or by society, in general, are solved through a series of efforts involving thinking and reasoning.

The powers of thinking and reasoning may thus be considered to be the essential tools for the welfare and meaningful existence of the individual as well as society.

CHAPTER SEVENTEEN

TYPES OF THINKING:

Thinking can be classified as follows:
1. Perceptual or Concrete Thinking:
This is the simplest form of thinking the basis of this type is perception, i.e. interpretation of sensation according to one's experience.
It is also called concrete thinking as it is carried out on the perception of actual or concrete objects and events.
2. Concept
dual or Abstract Thinking:
Here one makes use of concepts, generalized objects and languages, it is regarded as being superior to perceptual thinking as it economizes efforts in understanding and problem-solving.
3. Reflective Thinking:
This type of thinking aims in solving complex problems, thus it requires reorganization of all the relevant experiences to a situation or removing obstacles instead of relating with that experiences or ideas.

This is an insightful cognitive approach in reflective thinking as the mental activity here does not involve the mechanical trial and error type of effort.

In this type, thinking processes take all the relevant facts arranged in a logical order into account in order to arrive at a solution to the problem.

4. Creative Thinking:

This type of thinking is associated with one's ability to create or construct something new, novel or unusual.

It looks for new relationships and associations to describe and interpret the nature of things, events and situations.

Here the individual himself usually formulates the evidences and tools for its solution. For example; scientists, artists or inventors.

Skinner, the famous psychologist says creative thinking means that the prediction and inferences for the individual are new, original, ingenious and unusual.

The creative thinker is one who expresses new ideas and makes new observations, new predictions and new inferences.

Characteristics of Creative Thinking:

a. Creative thinking, in all its shapes and forms is absolutely an internal mental process and hence should be considered as an important component of one's cognitive behaviour.

b. Every one of us is capable of creative thinking and hence it is a universal phenomenon.

c. Creative thinking results in the production of something new or novel including a new form of arrangement of old elements.

d. Creative thinking in all its dimensions involves divergent thinking instead of the routine and final types of convergent thinking.

The mind must have complete freedom to wander around to create a new idea.

e. The field of creative thinking and its out part is quite comprehensive and built wide. It covers all the aspects of human accomplishments belonging to an individual's life.

5. Critical Thinking:

It is a type of thinking that helps a person in stepping aside from his own personal beliefs, prejudices and opinions to sort out the faiths and discover the truth, even at the expense of his basic belief system.

Here one resorts to set higher cognitive abilities and skills for the proper interpretation, analysis, evaluation, and inference, as well as explanation of the gathered or communicated information resulting in a purposeful unbiased, and self-regulatory judgment.

An ideal thinker is habitually inquisitive, well-informed, open-minded, flexible, fair-minded in evaluation, free from personal bias and prejudices, honest in seeking relevant information, skilled in the proper use of the abilities like interpretation, analysis, synthesis, evaluation, and drawing conclusion and inferences, etc.

The critical thinking is of a higher order well-disciplined thought process that involves the use of cognitive skills like conceptualization, interpretation, analysis, synthesis and evaluation for arriving at an unbiased, valid and reliable judgment of the gathered or communicated information or data as a guide to one's belief and action.

6. Non-directed or Associative Thinking:

There are times when we find ourselves engaged in a
unique type of thinking which is non-directed and
without a goal. It is reflected through dreaming and
other free-flowing uncontrolled activities.
Psychologically these forms of thought are termed as
associative thinking.
Here day-dreaming, fantasy and delusions all fall in
the category of withdrawal behaviour that helps an
individual to escape.
The demands of the real world by making his
thinking face non-directed and floating, placing him
somewhere, ordering something unconnected with his
environment.
We hear there is nothing seriously abnormal in
behaviour involving daydreaming and fantasy but
behaviour involving delusions definitely points towards
abnormality.
A person under the influence of such delusions may
think or believe that he is a millionaire, the ruler of the
universe, a great inventor, a noted historian or even God.
In contrast, a person in the grip of delusion may be
inclined to be the most incapable, unworthy and
unwanted person and may develop guilt feelings or
complain that he is the victim of some incurable physical
or mental diseases.

Development of Thinking:
Thinking is one of the most important aspects of
learning process. Our ability to learn and
solve the problems depends upon our ability to think
correctly which helps us in adjustment and is necessary
for a successful living.
Only those men who can think distinctly,
constructively and carefully can very much contribute

something worthwhile to the society.

As no person is born-thinker, one has to acquire knowledge of technique and practise of proper thinking. There are few methods which help to develop thinking through training.

1. Adequacy of the Knowledge and Experience:
Adequacy of the knowledge and experience is considered to be the background of systematic thinking.

So care should be taken to help the children with adequate knowledge and experiences which can be done by:

(a) Training the children to enhance the process of sensation and perception to gain better knowledge and experience to improve critical thinking.

(b) A person should be provided with opportunities for gaining adequate experiences and should be encouraged for self-study, discussion and participation in healthy and stimulating activities.

2. Adequate Motivation and Definiteness of Aims:
Motivation helps in mobilizing our energy for thinking. It creates genuine interest and voluntary attention in the process of thinking, and thus helps a lot in increasing the adequacy and efficiency of our thinking.

Thus one should try to think on definite lines with a definite end or purpose, the problems we solve should have intimate connection with our immediate needs and basic motives, and such thinking should be directed on creative and productive activities.

3. Adequate Freedom and Flexibility:
Thinking should not be obstructed by imposing unnecessary restrictions and narrowing of the field of thought process.

If the past experiences or habitual methods do not help in solving the problem we should strive for new association, relationships and possibilities for arriving at satisfactory results.

4. Incubation:

When we set ourselves to solve a problem but fail to solve it in-spite of our strain, putting more efforts into thinking and persistent thinking, it is better to lay aside the problem for some time and relax for a while or engage in some other activity.

During this interval a solution is evolved to that specific problem through the efforts of our unconscious mind. This phenomenon of incubation is helpful.

5. Intelligence and Wisdom:

Intelligence is defined as the ability to think properly, and thus proper development of intelligence is essential for bringing adequate thinking.

Proper care should be taken to use intelligence, wisdom and other cognitive abilities for carrying out the process of thinking.

6. Proper Development of Concepts and Language:

Concept is a word or idea with a generalized meaning which represents an entire class of objects, ideas, or events; for example, the word "saree" is a concept.

When you think of this word it represents all kinds of sarees which are six yards or eight yards long sarees made of silk, cotton, nylon or a mixture of the concept formation begins

in early childhood which are first hand face-to-face example. It can be +ve or -ve.

Language is a highly developed system of symbols in which words within a grammar can be written or spoken in different combinations.

Much of the thinking depends upon language although some imaging are also present.
Concepts, symbols, signs, words and language are the vehicles as well as instruments of thought.
Without their proper development one cannot proceed effectively on the path of thinking.
Their development stimulates and guides the thought process.
Improper development and faulty formation of concepts and likewise, symbolic behaviour not only hampers a person's progress in thinking but also proves fatal, as they may provoke perverted thinking and wrong conclusions.
7. Adequacy of Reasoning Process:
Thinking is also influenced by the mode of reasons one adopts. Illogical reasoning often leads to incorrect thinking.
Logic is the science of correct reasoning which helps to think correctly. Therefore, we should cultivate the habit of logical reasoning among our children.

CHAPTER EIGHTEEN

TOOLS OF THINKING:

There are a few important elements involved in the thinking process:

1.Images:

As mental pictures consist of personal experiences of objects, persons or situations, heard and felt.

These mental pictures symbolize actual objects, experiences and activities. In thinking, we usually manipulate the images rather than the actual objects, experiences or activities.

2. Concepts:

A concept is a general idea that stands for a general class and represents the common characteristics of all objects or events of this general class.

Concept, as a tool, economize the efforts in thinking, for example, when we hear the word 'elephant' we are at once reminded not only about the nature and qualities of elephant as a class but also our own experiences and understanding of them come to the surface in our consciousness to stimulate our thinking at that time.

1.   Symbols and signs:

Symbols and signs represent and stand for substitute of the actual objects, experiences and activities.
For example, traffic lights, railway signals, school bells, badges, songs, flags and slogans all are symbolic expressions, they stimulate and motivate resultant thinking because they tell us what to do or how to act.

1.   Language:

Is the most efficient and developed vehicle used for carrying out the process of thinking. When a person reads, writes or hears words or sentences or observes gesture in any language one is stimulated to think. Thus reading and writing of documents and literature also help in stimulating and promoting the thinking process.

3.   Muscular activities:

Thinking in one way or the other shows the evidence of the involvement of some incipient movements of groups of our muscles.
A high positive relation has been found to exist for the thinking and muscular activities of an individual. The more we engage ourselves in thought, the greater is the general muscular tension and conversely as we moved towards muscular relation, our thought processes gradually diminish.

4.   Brain functions:

Whatever may be the role of the muscles, thinking is primarily a function of the brain. Our mind is said to be the chief instrument of the thinking process.

The experiences registered by our sense organs have no meaning, and thus cannot serve as stimulating agents, or instruments for thinking unless these impressions are received by our brain cells and properly interpreted to derive some meaning.

The mental pictures or images can be stored, reconstructed or put to use only on being processed by the brain.

What happens in our thought process is simply the function or product of the activities of our brain.

Errors in Thinking:

Our thinking, reasoning, and problem-solving behavior all are largely influenced by our "sets", which is a kind of habit or a way in which we have accustomed ourselves to perceiving certain situations.

Whatever is registered earlier in our perceptions or experience provide side the base for our present and future thinking.

We won't change from our pre-set path of thinking which leads toward rigid behaviour.

We happen to make mistakes because of our attitude, likes and dislikes, bias or oversimplified thinking, reasoning and problem-solving, etc.

These mental sets have been gained from previous experiences surely interfere with our subsequent thinking resulting in ineffective behaviour.

Thus our thinking will be defective and harmful if it is not based on correct data or information.

Our biases, prejudices and beliefs sometimes do not enable us to think logically.

We make wrong conclusion because of our prejudices, hence we are inclined to ignore and overlook those facts which support right conclusion.

Our thinking is defective because we have allowed ourselves to be swayed by our emotions.

Many people do not think clearly and accurately during an examination because they have been disturbed by fear and failure.

Many times our thinking become fallacious, and cannot view the problem from different angles broadly.

Many of our thinking may also be distorted by superstitions or by lack of information that is relevant to the subject.

Many of our wishful thinking are also unscientific thinking.

Our prejudices and biases cause conflicts, rationalizations and delusions which are defective thinking as well.

The more you want to be simple in your life , it shall actually make your life more complicated!!(Source from a closed person)